GH NO
1

D0295919

A FOCUS ON...

ANXIETY & DEPRESSION

©2018
Book Life
King's Lynn
Norfolk PE30 4LS

ISBN: 9781786372314

All rights reserved
Printed in Malaysia

Written by:
Charlie Ogden

Edited by:
Kirsty Holmes

Designed by:
Daniel Scase

A catalogue record for this book
is available from the British Library.

CONTENTS

Words that look like **this** are explained in the glossary on **PAGE 31.**

WORRY AND ANXIETY

Anxiety is a type of **emotion** and it is similar to feeling worried. When people feel very worried, they are said to feel anxious. Anxiety also sometimes feels similar to fear. However, the two emotions are slightly different. Fear is a **reaction** to a threat or event that is actually happening. Anxiety is a reaction to a threat or event that might happen in the future.

People who feel worried often behave in unusual ways. They might walk back and forth across a room, tap their feet on the ground or bite their fingernails. These are known as nervous behaviours. As well as this, people who are worried often feel tired, have trouble concentrating and have the feeling of butterflies in their stomach.

When people feel scared, they are often scared of a **specific** thing or event. A person might get scared by a mouse that just ran across their bedroom floor or a spooky noise that is coming from upstairs. Feeling anxious is different. Your worry is more **general.**

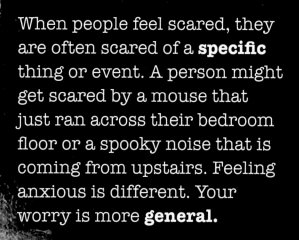

For example, someone going to a new school might be anxious about meeting all their new classmates. In this example, the person probably doesn't think that something specific will go wrong, such as accidentally calling the teacher 'Dad' or falling over in front of the whole class. Instead, they are more likely to be worried that something, anything, might go wrong.

ANXIETY IS A COMMON HUMAN EMOTION AND EVERYBODY FEELS ANXIOUS FROM TIME TO TIME.

TYPES OF ANXIETY

There are different types of anxiety. Many types of anxiety are related to specific events, but others are more general. Some of the most common types of anxiety are explained here.

PERFORMANCE ANXIETY

When we feel like an event needs to go well, like a sports match or a presentation at school, we often get worried. This is because we want to do well and are worried about what will happen if we don't. This type of worry is called 'performance anxiety'.

Performance anxiety is sometimes called 'test anxiety' because people often feel like this before a test or exam. This is because tests and exams are used to measure a person's skill and see how much they can remember about a subject. People often feel that it is important to do well in exams, which can make them feel anxious about performing badly.

FACT ⚡

THESE TYPES OF ANXIETY ARE USUALLY COMPLETELY NORMAL. HOWEVER, IF YOUR FEELINGS OF WORRY ARE STOPPING YOU FROM DOING THINGS YOU ENJOY, IT MAY BE THAT YOU ARE experiencing CLINICAL ANXIETY. FIND OUT MORE ABOUT THIS ON PAGE 12.

STAGE FRIGHT

Stage fright is another type of anxiety that lots of people experience. We feel stage fright when we are about to go in front of a crowd of people. For example, you might feel stage fright before going onstage in a school play, or being filmed with a camera.

People feel stage fright because they are worried that if something goes wrong, then lots of people will see and know about it. Stage fright can make people feel very nervous about being in front of a crowd. However, most people find that their stage fright goes away once they are on stage.

SOCIAL ANXIETY

Social anxiety is the worried and uneasy feeling that people sometimes have before important social events. A social event is any time that a lot of people, usually families and friends, all meet up. Often, social events are places to have fun.

Important social events, such as weddings, can make us anxious because lots of our friends and family will be there. We want to look and act our best in front of these people. Social anxiety can make people worried before a social event, but usually goes away once they get there and start having a good time.

SADNESS AND DEPRESSION

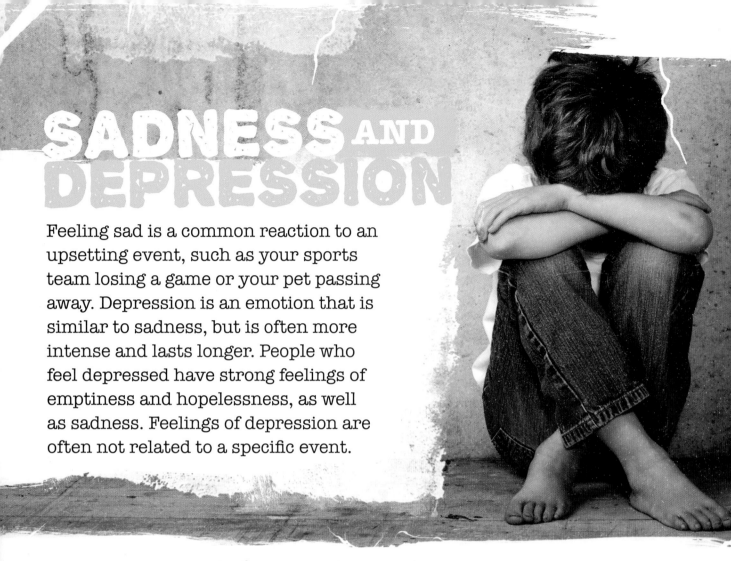

Feeling sad is a common reaction to an upsetting event, such as your sports team losing a game or your pet passing away. Depression is an emotion that is similar to sadness, but is often more intense and lasts longer. People who feel depressed have strong feelings of emptiness and hopelessness, as well as sadness. Feelings of depression are often not related to a specific event.

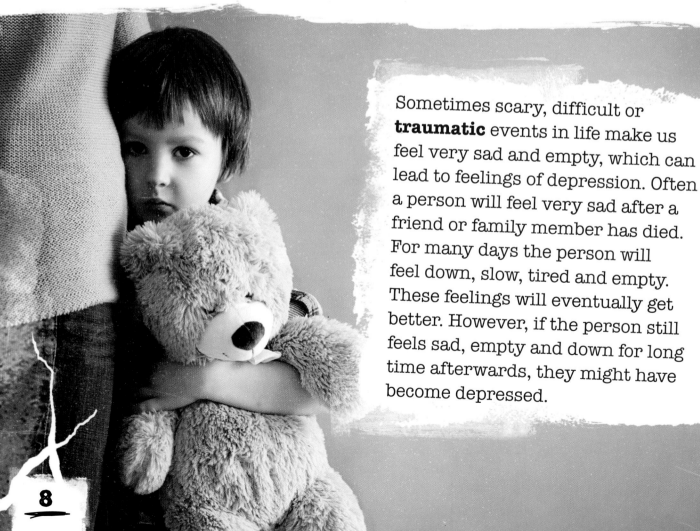

Sometimes scary, difficult or **traumatic** events in life make us feel very sad and empty, which can lead to feelings of depression. Often a person will feel very sad after a friend or family member has died. For many days the person will feel down, slow, tired and empty. These feelings will eventually get better. However, if the person still feels sad, empty and down for long time afterwards, they might have become depressed.

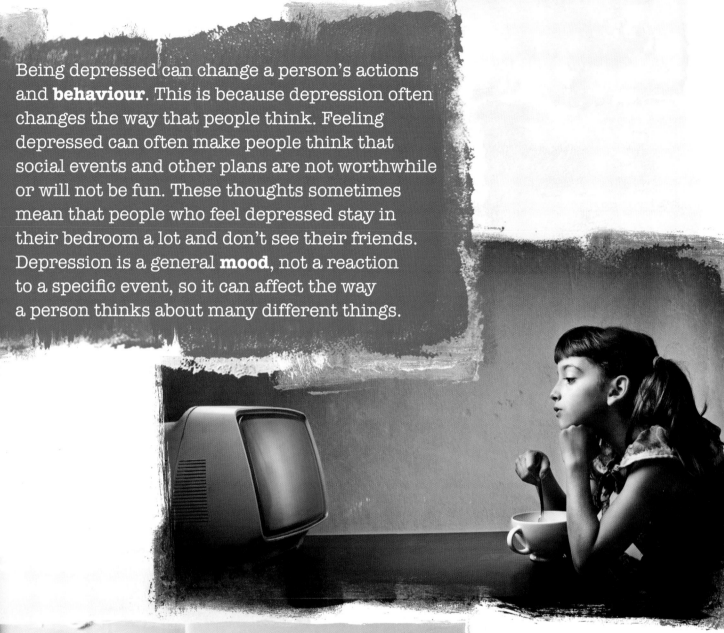

Being depressed can change a person's actions and **behaviour**. This is because depression often changes the way that people think. Feeling depressed can often make people think that social events and other plans are not worthwhile or will not be fun. These thoughts sometimes mean that people who feel depressed stay in their bedroom a lot and don't see their friends. Depression is a general **mood**, not a reaction to a specific event, so it can affect the way a person thinks about many different things.

When people feel depressed, they often feel tired and slow. Depressed people might stay in bed for longer than usual and be unable to concentrate at work or school. Things that used to make them happy and lively, such as sports or music, might not affect them in the same way.

FACT

FEELINGS OF SADNESS CAN BE VERY UNPLEASANT, BUT THEY ARE A COMMON REACTION TO A DIFFICULT TIME IN LIFE AND USUALLY GO AWAY IN TIME.

DIFFICULT EMOTIONS

Worry and sadness are both normal human emotions and everyone will feel worried and sad at some point in their life. Feeling sad or worried can even help a person to deal with a stressful part of their life. Because of this, we can say that there are times when it is normal and healthy to feel these emotions.

FACT

SADNESS AND WORRY SHOULD ONLY HAPPEN FROM TIME TO TIME, AND IT'S OK TO FEEL SAD WHEN SOMETHING UPSETTING HAPPENS.

FEELING SAD

Feeling sad is a common reaction to a stressful or difficult time in life. Things can happen to upset you at home, at school, or in other parts of your life. However, as time passes and life becomes easier and less stressful, these feelings of sadness should go away. Having feelings of sadness like this is totally normal.

People often feel sad when there is **trauma** in their life. For example, people who are bullied often feel sad. The emotions that these people feel are normal because being bullied is stressful and upsetting. However, having to deal with bullying is not normal. When a person is sad, it is important to think about what is causing their sadness to see if it can be stopped.

FEELING WORRIED

Feeling worried is a common reaction to stressful and important events that are going to happen in the future. Events such as doing a presentation at school or a big change, like moving to a new home, often make people feel worried. People who feel worried in these situations might get very nervous and think about the event a lot before it happens. However, normal worrying does not stop people from doing things that they know are important.

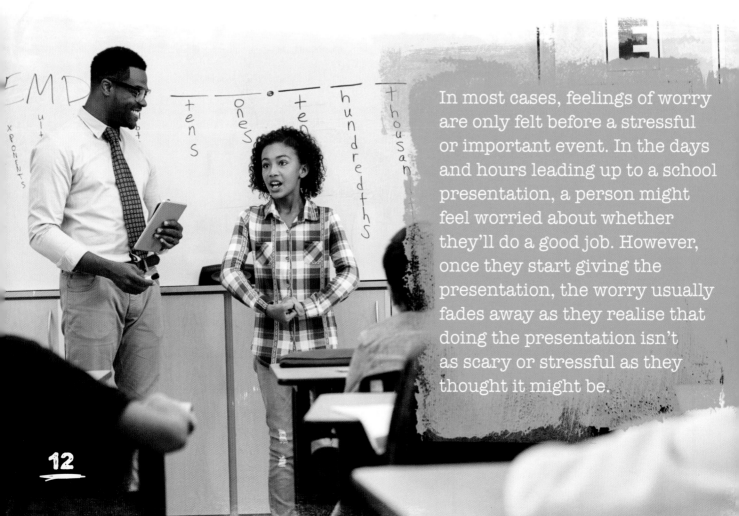

In most cases, feelings of worry are only felt before a stressful or important event. In the days and hours leading up to a school presentation, a person might feel worried about whether they'll do a good job. However, once they start giving the presentation, the worry usually fades away as they realise that doing the presentation isn't as scary or stressful as they thought it might be.

Being worried can also affect the body. The most common way that worry affects the body are by giving a person the feeling of butterflies in their stomach, making a person's heart beat faster and their hands sweaty. These **physical** reactions are usually a little uncomfortable, but are common effects of worry.

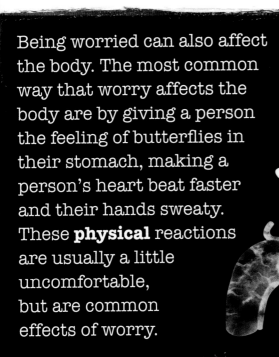

PHYSICAL SYMPTOMS

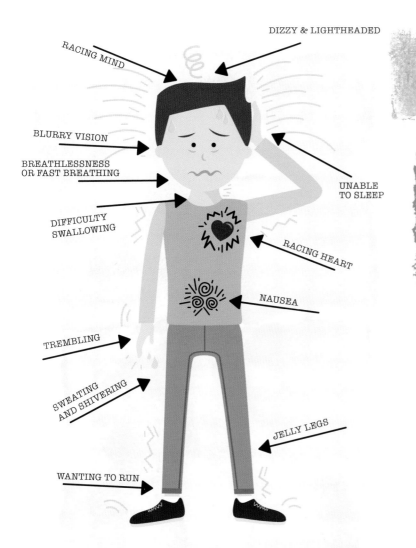

RACING MIND

DIZZY & LIGHTHEADED

BLURRY VISION

BREATHLESSNESS OR FAST BREATHING

DIFFICULTY SWALLOWING

UNABLE TO SLEEP

RACING HEART

NAUSEA

TREMBLING

SWEATING AND SHIVERING

JELLY LEGS

WANTING TO RUN

Worry and anxiety can both affect the body. However, the way our body responds to each emotion can be different, and each person can feel different things. The way that the body reacts to anxiety can sometimes be used to identify a person with an anxiety **disorder.** Look at the diagram to see some of the most common physical reactions to anxiety.

CLINICAL ANXIETY

Some people's feelings of anxiety are much stronger than others. They might be anxious about things that are unlikely to happen, or everyday events. These people feel anxious much more often than usual and their anxiety is usually a lot more extreme. People who have this kind of anxiety are usually said to have clinical anxiety or an anxiety disorder.

PANIC ATTACKS: Panic attacks can be part of an anxiety disorder. They feel frightening but are actually harmless. When a person has a panic attack, they suddenly feel very afraid, and may have scary physical symptoms like fast breathing or a pounding heart . Panic attacks can be controlled with slow breathing and other techniques.

People with anxiety disorders usually find that their anxiety affects their day-to-day life. Their feelings of anxiety are **triggered** on a daily basis and sometimes stop them from being able to do all the things they want to. Having an anxiety disorder can make life difficult, but there are now lots of **treatments** that can help people with anxiety disorders to live happy, normal lives.

FIGHT FLIGHT FREEZE RESPONSE

Feelings of anxiety can be partly explained by the Fight, Flight, Freeze (FFF) response. When we face a threatening situation, the body uses the FFF response to protect itself from whatever the threat may be. When our FFF response is triggered, we get a rush of energy, our hearts start beating faster and our minds race to try to work out ways to avoid the threat.

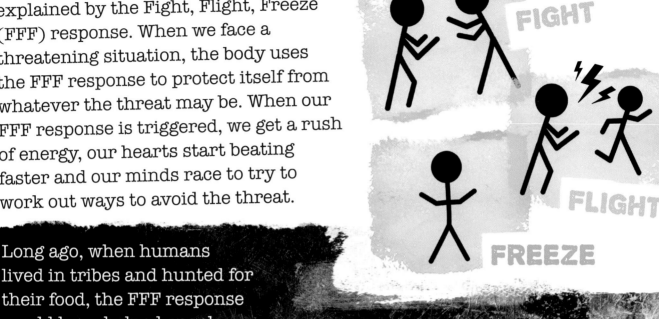

Long ago, when humans lived in tribes and hunted for their food, the FFF response would have helped people. For example, if a person was threatened by a wild animal, the extra energy and the quick thinking could help them to fight off the animal or run away from it fast enough to escape.

Today, this response can be used to explain the physical feelings of anxiety. When people feel threatened by a future event, their FFF kicks in and causes many of the physical effects of anxiety, such as a racing, confused mind, or feeling trapped or frozen. Experts believe that many people with anxiety disorders experience the FFF response more often than other people.

FACT THIS CAN BE THE BODY'S WAY OF TESTING IT'S EMERGENCY RESPONSES, EVEN WHEN THERE IS NO EMERGENCY. THINK OF IT AS A FIRE DRILL FOR YOUR BODY!

ANXIETY DISORDERS

There are many different kinds of anxiety disorder. Anxiety disorders often relate to the specific events that trigger a person's FFF response, which then leads to the feelings of anxiety. Some of the most common anxiety disorders are explained here.

SEPARATION ANXIETY DISORDERS

People often feel **homesick** when they leave home for a long time. Separation anxiety is different – people with this disorder have very strong feelings of anxiety when they are separated from their home or family. They feel nervous, shaky and sick. They may also be scared that something bad will soon happen if they don't get back to their house or family. This can make it difficult for people with separation anxiety disorder to go to school or have fun with their friends at social events.

SOCIAL ANXIETY DISORDERS

People with social anxiety disorder get strong feelings of anxiety before and during social situations. People with this disorder usually have their FFF response triggered by one or two specific social situations, such as talking to strangers or talking in front of a group. This can cause sweating, blushing, **nausea** and shaking, on top of the normal feelings of anxiety. People with social anxiety often avoid social situations because the feelings of anxiety that they experience are too unpleasant. This can make things like going to school with social anxiety very difficult and lonely.

FACT

MOST PEOPLE WHO HAVE THIS DISORDER START NOTICING IT BETWEEN THE AGES OF 8 AND 15. IF YOU FEEL THIS WAY, TALK TO AN ADULT YOU TRUST WHO CAN HELP YOU.

GENERALISED ANXIETY DISORDERS

People with generalised anxiety disorder regularly worry about things in life, like their health, school work and their family. This disorder can give people headaches, stomach pains and nausea and can often make people feel angry and tired. When worrying about things stops a person from enjoying their daily life, it can be a sign that they have generalised anxiety disorder.

FACT

ANXIETY DISORDERS ARE VERY COMMON. ESTIMATES STATE THAT 10-40% OF PEOPLE WILL DEVELOP AN ANXIETY DISORDER AT SOME POINT IN THEIR LIFE.

CLINICAL DEPRESSION

Usually, feelings of depression are usually caused by a traumatic or upsetting event and then slowly fade over time. The event may still be upsetting to think about, but it gets accepted and life moves forward. People with clinical depression, however, might get strong feelings of depression for a long time after a traumatic or upsetting event.

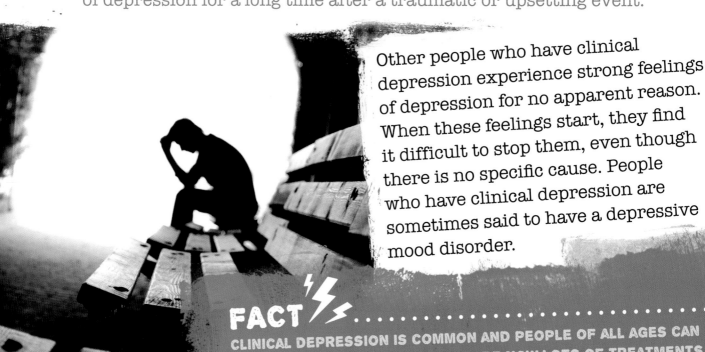

Other people who have clinical depression experience strong feelings of depression for no apparent reason. When these feelings start, they find it difficult to stop them, even though there is no specific cause. People who have clinical depression are sometimes said to have a depressive mood disorder.

FACT

CLINICAL DEPRESSION IS COMMON AND PEOPLE OF ALL AGES CAN EXPERIENCE IT. HOWEVER, THERE ARE NOW LOTS OF TREATMENTS TO HELP THOSE WITH CLINICAL DEPRESSION. FIND OUT MORE ABOUT TREATING CLINICAL DEPRESSION ON PAGE 24.

While most people experience feelings of depression for a few days or weeks after a traumatic or upsetting event, people with clinical depression can feel depressed for months or years at a time. Having clinical depression can also affect a person's body and make them feel unwell. Getting past these depressed feelings is very difficult without treatment.

People with clinical depression are often said to have 'episodes' of depression. A depressive episode is when someone with a depressive mood disorder becomes very depressed, very quickly – usually for no specific reason. Episodes can last a long time, sometimes months, and can end just as quickly as they started. These episodes can happen at any time, and can be treated with counselling or medication.

EFFECTS OF CLINICAL DEPRESSION

Clinical depression causes extreme feelings of sadness and hopelessness. This is because depression is an illness, so it affects the mind, and also the body too.

TIREDNESS

People with clinical depression can feel constantly tired. Their limbs often feel heavy, their mind can be clouded and they might sleep for much longer than usual.

CHANGES IN APPETITE

Sometimes, people with clinical depression eat more or less than usual. They may also feel like they have no energy, and find it difficult to get **motivated**. This means they can lose or gain weight as their **appetite** changes.

FACT
STUDIES SHOW THAT EXERCISING CAN HELP TO REDUCE FEELINGS OF DEPRESSION.

APATHY

People in a depressive episode often find it hard to be interested in things that they used to enjoy. This is called apathy. Music, sports and even friendships can become dull and uninteresting to people with clinical depression. When people experience strong feelings of apathy towards everything, they might feel like they can't face seeing friends or getting out of bed or may even stop eating regular meals. This can be very dangerous and may affect the person's health. With treatment and time, this will often get better.

MOOD SWINGS

Other people with clinical depression experience mood swings. This means that they experience very strong emotions. People who are affected by clinical depression in this way often switch between emotions very quickly, one minute being very angry and the next being very sad. People who experience mood swings can find that they are stressed and emotional in lots of situations and this can make it hard for them to have friendships and feel happy.

RECOGNISING ANXIETY AND DEPRESSION

Anxiety and depression come in degrees – they can be felt a little, a medium amount or a lot. Some people have very **severe** anxiety or depression, meaning that their disorder makes life very difficult for them and they nearly always feel anxious or depressed. Other people, however, have disorders that impact on their lives much less. Most of the time, these people are not anxious or depressed. However, when they do feel sad or anxious, it is often very intense. Recognising whether you suffer from clinical anxiety or depression is always important, whether your disorder is severe or not.

Sometimes people don't know that they have clinical anxiety or depression. This may simply be because their disorder is not very severe. While the disorder will still affect their life now and then, they may have learnt to live with the disorder. They may even believe that it is a normal part of life. Other people, however, may struggle with strong feelings of anxiety and depression, but still not recognise them as a disorder. These people often try to manage their disorder by themselves, which can sometimes make the problem worse.

FACT.....................
SOME PEOPLE MAY APPEAR HAPPY, BUT ACTUALLY FEEL ANXIOUS OR DEPRESSED.

It is important for a person who feels any degree of anxiety or depression to recognise that they feel this way, and get some support. These disorders are very common and by recognising a problem, a person can begin to make **positive** changes in their life. With treatment, symptoms related to anxiety and depression often get much better over time. If feelings of sadness or worry are stopping you from doing things, or enjoying things you usually like, talk to an adult that you trust, who will help you.

It's important to talk about your feelings. If you keep them to yourself, common feelings of worry or anxiety can build up, and become more of a problem. Sharing them can help you feel better right away. If you think a friend, or someone in your class, might be feeling this way, ask them if they would like to talk to you. This can help them to feel supported and to feel better.

TREATING ANXIETY AND DEPRESSION

Most people who receive treatment for their anxiety or depression notice that their disorder gets better and many people are able to almost completely get rid of their disorder. There are now a range of treatments for people with anxiety and depression to choose from, meaning that most people are able to find a treatment that works for them.

Some of the most **effective** treatments for anxiety and depression are talking treatments. This involves a person talking to a **professional** about the emotions they've been feeling. Having counselling, or talking to a doctor often helps the counsellor to work out some of the things that make a person anxious or depressed. They will explain how these feelings can affect their thoughts and behaviours. They can also suggest ways to help fight off strong feelings of anxiety and depression.

Treatments for anxiety and depression often involve a combination of breathing and muscle exercises. Breathing exercises involve breathing in a special way to help you to feel calm. Muscle exercises involve tensing and relaxing your muscles and can help to relax the body. These exercises are very simple and usually only take a few minutes to complete.

SLOW, SMOOTH BREATHING

Some of the most effective breathing exercises fortreating anxiety involve slow, steady breathing. Doing these exercises two or three times a day can help to reduce a person's feelings of anxiety. To try this, follow the steps below:

1. Breathe in through your nose for a count of four. Keep your breathing slow and smooth.
2. Hold for one or two seconds.
3. Breathe out through your mouth for a count of five. Keep your breathing slow and smooth.
4. Wait for two seconds.
5. Repeat until you feel calm and less anxious.

TOP TIP

TALKING TREATMENTS AND EXERCISES CAN SOMETIMES TAKE TIME TO WORK. HOWEVER, MOST PEOPLE WHO CONTINUE WITH THEIR TREATMENT FIND THAT THEY SOON START TO FEEL MORE CALM AND LESS WORRIED.

REPEAT UNTIL YOU FEEL CALM

0.4   0.2   0.5   0.2

FACT
A DOCTOR MAY ALSO PRESCRIBE MEDICATION TO HELP WITH THEIR ANXIETY AND DEPRESSION.

ANXIETY AND DEPRESSION TODAY

For most of human history, doctors and scientists did not study anxiety or depression in much detail. In the last few decades, more scientific studies have been done about anxiety and depression. Now that doctors are better at diagnosing clinical anxiety and depression, more people are able to get the treatment they need for their disorder. This has helped to improve the lives of millions of people.

FACT

OVER 10 MILLION PEOPLE RECEIVE TREATMENT FOR ANXIETY OR DEPRESSION IN THE U.S.A. ALONE. HOWEVER, EXPERTS BELIEVE THAT MANY OF THESE PEOPLE DON'T LOOK FOR TREATMENT.

FACT

ONE IN SIX ADULTS IN THE U.K. AND U.S.A., OR OVER 50 MILLION PEOPLE, ARE NOW AFFECTED BY AN ANXIETY DISORDER.

YOU ARE NOT ALONE

If you think you or someone you know might be suffering with anxiety or depression, it is important to know that you are not the only one. These feelings are very common, and there is lots of help available.

FACT ⚡⚡
DEPRESSION WILL AFFECT ABOUT ONE IN TEN PEOPLE AT SOME POINT DURING THEIR LIFE.

FACT ⚡⚡
DEPRESSION IS THE MOST COMMON MENTAL HEALTH PROBLEM IN THE WORLD, FOLLOWED BY ANXIETY.

FACT ⚡⚡
STUDIES SHOW THAT AROUND 4% OF CHILDREN IN THE U.K. RIGHT NOW HAVE PROBLEMS WITH ANXIETY OR DEPRESSION.

FACT ⚡⚡
ANXIETY AND DEPRESSION DISORDERS ARE SOME OF THE MOST COMMON ILLNESSES IN THE U.K AND THE U.S.A.

ANXIETY AND DEPRESSION IN THE U.S.A AND EUROPE

Scientific studies about anxiety and depression have been done in lots of countries around the world. From these studies, we can see that anxiety and depression affects every country and **society** in the world. However, they also seem to show that people who live in the U.S.A. or Europe are more likely to suffer from severe anxiety disorders and depressive mood disorders. Why could that be?

People in these countries can feel pressured to be interested in things like money, and how they look. Many doctors and scientists believe that this could be part of the reason why there is a higher amount of clinical depression and anxiety in these places. Doctors believe that this can make people feel bad about themselves because they aren't rich enough, popular enough or attractive enough. These thoughts can then lead to anxiety and depression in a lot of people.

28

Most people in America and Europe own either a mobile phone, a computer, a television or a games console. Lots of people own all four of these things. While these technologies are brilliant, and help us communicate, too much time spent on them instead of with family and friends can lead to people feeling lonely. Because of this, these people could have weaker **relationships** with others around them than is usual. This may make them more likely to suffer from anxiety or depression.

People who use social media sites see a lot of pictures and videos of people doing fun and fantastic things. They don't, however, see any videos of people doing any of the normal, day-to-day things. This can make people think that other people's lives are more fun and exciting than theirs, which can make them feel anxious or depressed.

FACT

YOU CAN ALSO FIND HELP, INFORMATION AND SUPPORT ONLINE.

FIND OUT MORE

USE THE LINKS BELOW TO FIND OUT MORE ABOUT ANXIETY AND DEPRESSION.

http://www.nhs.uk/conditions/depression

https://www.anxietyuk.org.uk

https://youngminds.org.uk

http://www.worrywisekids.org

If you have any questions about anxiety or depression that can't be answered by using these links, it is best to ask an adult you trust or a doctor first.

GLOSSARY

appetite feeling hungry, and how much a person likes to eat

behaviour the way a person acts or behaves.

counselling talking to person who gives professional advice.

disorder a physical or mental sickness or ailment.

effective able to make happen or change something, works well.

emotion a strong feeling such as joy, hatred, sorrow, or fear.

experience something that a person has done or lived through.

general relating to all or most of something or of some group; not limited to any particular thing or member.

homesick distress or sadness felt when someone has to leave their home, for a long or short time

mood the way a person feels at a certain time.

motivated feeling a strong desire to do something

nausea a sick feeling in the stomach with the need to vomit

negative not helpful or constructive.

physical effects when a medication or outside influence changes something in the body

positive something good or optimistic

professional of or having to do with a certain job or work

reaction an action or response to something that has happened or has been done.

relationships connections between people.

scientific studies a study conducted using scientific methods to determine an outcome

severe (of something bad) serious, very great or intense

society a collection people living together in a group of communities

specific exact and precise

symptoms something that happens in the body suggesting that there is a disease or disorder.

trauma an emotional shock that has a deep effect on one's life for a long time.

traumatic having to do with a trauma

treatment giving medicine or using other ways to help cure a disease or heal an injury

triggered when something sets off a feeling of anxiety or depression

INDEX

PHOTO CREDITS

Photocredits: Abbreviations: l-left, r-right, b-bottom, t-top, c-centre, m-middle.
Front Cover – Ljupco Smokovski, 2 – Evgeny Atamanenko, 4 – pathdoc, 4b – spillikin, 5t – prapass, 5m – Szasz-Fabian Jozsef, 5b – Monkey Business Images, 6t – baranq, 6m – Chinnapong, 7t – aerogondo2, 7b – italay, 8t – Suzanne Tucker, 8b – Tomsickova Tatyana, 9m – Ollyy, 9b – Chinnabong, 10t – michaeljung, 10m – Monkey Business Images, 10l – Monkey Business Images, 10r – michaeljung, 11t – Intellistudies, 11r – Tom Wang, 12r – Mindmo, 12b – Monkey Business Images, 13t – Catherine Glazkova, 13r – ruigsantos, 13b – Fancy Tapis, 14t – Fabrik Bilder, 14b – Photographee.eu, 15m – Circlephoto, 15b – pathdoc, 16t – Studio 10ne, 16b – Ollyy 17 – Peerayot, 18t – Charles taylor, 18b – hikrcn, 19t – toeytoey, 19b – Jan Faukner, 20t – Koldunov, 20b – Pumidol, 21t – liza54500, 21b – Lopolo, 22t – liza54500, 22b – ra2studio, 23t – wavebreakmedia, 23m – George Rudy, 23b – Monkey Business Images, 24t – Monkey Business Images, 24m – Photographee.eu, 24b – Monkey Business Images, 25t – fizkes, 25r – file404, 25b – Fancy Tapis, 26t – eakkaluktemwanich, 26r – VaLiza, 26b – Monkey Business Images, 27 – Stokkete, 28t – oneinchpunch, 28m – Andrea Raffin, 29t – Twin Design, 29r – Refat, 29l – tanuha2001, 29b – M-SUR.
Images are courtesy of Shutterstock.com. With thanks to Getty Images, Thinkstock Photo and iStockphoto.